How To Study
Your Bible

How To Study Your Bible

Three Steps to Personal Bible Study

Rubens Ruba

© 2017 Rubens Ruba
All rights reserved.

ISBN: 1546813977
ISBN 13: 9781546813972

Dedicated to the Pastors and Leaders of Lewisburg Alliance Church

*Thank you for the last thirteen years that I have
had the privilege to be your Pastor.
Looking for God to do great things in the future at
LAC as we continue to minister together.*

*May each of you desire God's Word more than silver
and gold, finding it sweeter than honey.*

Table of Contents

Part 1	Introduction	1
Lesson 1	Why People Don't Study The Bible	5
Lesson 2	Why Study The Bible	12
Lesson 3	Who Can Study The Bible	16
Lesson 4	Can Your Trust The 66 Books In Our Bible?	25
Lesson 5	Is The Bible Really Necessary To Know God	39
Lesson 6	Today - Is The Bible Enough For Us?	51
Part 2	Three Steps To Studying The Bible	61
Lesson 7	Step One - Observation	63
Lesson 8	Step Two - Interpretation	69
Lesson 9	Step Three – Application	79
Lesson 10	Applying God's Word – Staying Away From Extremism	86
	Final Thoughts A Call For A New Reformation	93

PART 1

INTRODUCTION

For more than 47 years I have grown to love the Bible and to gain an understanding of its meaning. Therefore, the purpose of my writing this book is to help you do the same.

I'd like to first explain why I have grown to love the Word of God as much as I do. As early as I can remember, my parents had a great respect for God's Word. Each evening our family, made up of my three brothers and one sister, would gather around the dinner table, where Dad would read a portion of God's Word and then we would kneel as a family and pray. Further, they used the Scriptures in guiding our decisions. They used them as a constant guideline for everything that we did as children, but the Scriptures were also modeled before us.

Because God's Word was our domestic foundation, respect for God's Word was both expected and required. At the same time, we were allowed to challenge God's Word when it didn't make sense to us. Yet arguments and fights in the Ruba household didn't last long, because they were dealt with the Bible's method for crisis management. But please don't picture that our family was ruled with an iron fist. On the contrary, ours was a happy and peaceful home. There was a lot of laughter and still today our family is close, even though we may live a great distance away from each other.

It was in my senior year at Cedar Grove Christian Academy in Philadelphia, where I sensed God calling me into the ministry. People have asked me how I knew my calling. Well, it actually came through an individual desire to study the Scriptures. Then, during my High School years I started taking notes during sermons, instead of just listening to them. I began to listen to the radio teachers such as Charles Swindoll, David Jeremiah, and Charles Stanley. I really loved studying the Bible. The other way that God confirmed my calling came through some very godly men in my own church. Various people came up to me when I spoke and quietly stated that maybe I should consider the ministry. But the greatest influences in my life were my parents, brothers and sister. They were my greatest encouragement during those decision-making years.

Having grown up in that type of environment, I wanted to choose a spouse with similar values. When Beth and I met, I instantly knew that she was the one for me. Ten months later, we were married and she has shown me time and time again her commitment to God's Word. Throughout our marriage we have shared a high respect for God's Word. We've read God's Word and even hosted Bible studies in our home. Many times, we would share throughout the week what we learned about God and His Word. Her depth in God's Word is remarkable! She puts me to shame.

HOW TO STUDY YOUR BIBLE

As our daughters have grown up in our home, we have tried to instill in them the depth of God's Word and our prayer for them is that they, along with their husbands, will continue to not only "walk" the Christian life, but also to "grow deeper" by studying the Bible, God's Holy Word.

When it was time to pick a college, I chose Philadelphia College of Bible (now named Cairn University). During that time, I was exposed to the teaching of Dr. John Cawood, Dr. Renald Showers and Dr. James McGahey. One of the most beneficial courses, among many, that affected my thinking was on the subject of Bible Study methods. Even though I went to church all my life and loved to study God's Word, I came to realize how inadequate my approach to the Scriptures had been. During those classes at Philadelphia College of Bible, the principles of interpretation and application were so drilled into me that they have stayed with me for over thirty-seven years.

This personal history brings me full circle to the reason I am writing this book. I want to share those principles that I've learned through the years with each reader. As a result of your learning and application, my prayer is that you will grow in understanding the Word of God, without fear or intimidation.

The process of getting these principles into your mind is the calling of a Pastor. In 2 Timothy, the Apostle wrote these words in his latter years of ministry. He said, *"And the things you have heard me say in the presence of many witnesses entrust to reliable people who will also be qualified to teach others* (2 Timothy 2:2)."

It is my greatest desire that you will be well equipped to study the Word of God on your own and be prepared to pass it on to other "reliable people."

LESSON 1

WHY PEOPLE DON'T STUDY THE BIBLE

RIGHT AFTER I became a believer in Christ, I was given a Bible by my brother Claudio, and in it he wrote these words: "*This book will keep you from sin, or sin will keep you from this book.*" That was true then and it certainly is true now. Another way of saying it was: "*Dusty Bibles always lead to dirty lives.*" In fact, today you are either in the Word and the Word is conforming you into the image of Christ or you are <u>not</u> in the Word and the world is squeezing you into its mold. During times in my life when I have rebelled against God, I have thought about those true statements.

The tragedy among Christians today is that too many of us desire God's Word in our lives, but are not really into God's Word daily. I am amazed when people go across the country to hear a preacher, but personally (daily) they are not into God's Word. In other words, they are willing to go across the country to hear a famous pastor preach, but at the same time, they are not willing to go across the living room to pick up the Bible for themselves.

There's no question that Christians should go to conferences and hear different preachers. But that ought to be a stimulus and not a substitute for getting into God's Word.

Barna Research Group reported that in a typical week, only 10% of Americans read the Bible everyday. And even that figure may be high according to the president of Barna Group. Another survey found that 82% of Americans believe the Bible is true and "inspired" of God. Yet, half of those respondents could not name even one of the four gospel authors (Matthew, Mark, Luke and John). And even fewer than those could not share who delivered the Sermon on the Mount (Jesus).

Puzzling Questions

These days, with the increased movement to have Bibles on-line, I really wonder how many people are truly studying God's Word on a daily basis? Even though the Bible is more accessible, I just wonder if we are, as a Christian Church, becoming functionally illiterate six out of the seven days of the week.

Christians today have bought Bibles, read them on occasion, and even taken them to church, but it is still a struggle, despite the opportunities available, to study God's Word.

But why? Why is it that people do not get into the Scriptures on a daily basis? Let's look at <u>six reasons</u>, using <u>fictional examples of people</u> who don't study the Bible.

1. The Problem Of Relevance

"John" represents a very focused group of people in the Church. He has a lot of responsibility and acknowledges that he should study God's Word. Yet, he feels that the Bible is somewhat archaic. John states, "When you work in the public sector, you are up against things that aren't mentioned in the Bible. So, it doesn't exactly apply to your day-to-day situations."

John has summarized the problem of "relevance." This may be the top reason why people don't study God's Word. They use words such as "archaic, out-of-date and old fashioned" to describe this serious problem. Yet, as we will see, God's revelation is as alive today as it was when it was first delivered.

2. The Problem Of Methodology

"Sadie" is one among many in the Church who struggle with this area. She is a great academic with advanced degrees, but when it comes to God's Word, she states, "I've tried to study the Bible, but I can't do it. I don't know Hebrew or Greek and I just don't understand certain parts of the Bible."

Sadie's problem is that she lacks a method of studying the Scriptures. This is a common problem for many people. They don't want to "jump in" because they are afraid of drowning. Our culture doesn't help very much. With the increased dependence on *"Google search"* to acquire quick answers, we are losing our ability to read and to reason.

3. The Problem of False Humility

"Andrew" is meticulous and has an incredible work ethic in his job. If you have a problem and don't want to call a repairman because it's too expensive, Andrew is the one you want to call. He is the person who may not know initially how to fix something, but he will spend time studying in order to figure it out. Yet, when it comes to God's Word, he says, "I try to study God's Word, but after a while I wind up only studying what I understand such as The Ten Commandments, The Golden Rule and the Lord is our Shepherd type of passages.

There are a number of people who are just like Andrew. They only practice the truths in the Bible that they already understand. They say, "I'm just a layperson, or I'm just a housewife. I'm not a professional. I have no theological training." As we're going to see, you really don't need professional training to understand the Bible. You don't need to know Greek or Hebrew. As long as you can read, you can dig into God's Word.

4. The Problem of Priorities

"Lillian" is a homemaker. She's at home with four small children and her problem is when to find the time to study the Bible. She states, "I've tried to do it, but I have four small children, and sometimes I'd do anything to just get a break. My husband works during the day, and by evening we both are exhausted. I would do anything for a break most days.

This is a really hard issue because it has nothing to do with ability or methodology or even desire. It is the problem of priorities. Where does Bible study fit into the life of a busy mom? For most of us, we usually place it on the bottom of the priorities list. We approach it as a nice thing to do, but not exactly necessary. In the next section of this book we'll deal with whether Bible study is essential.

5. The Problem of Skepticism

"Walt" is a university student on a secular university campus. Walt says this about the Bible: "Yes, I suppose people should read and study the Bible. But I'm not sure that some of the miracles and predictions in the Bible are legitimate. Come on – Jonah and the whale? Or how about the flood? I'm not sure that I can accept the Bible as a consistent, real Word that comes from God.

These concerns that are raised by Walt are legitimate. Is the Bible reliable? Is it authoritative? Can we base our lives on it? Does it have credibility, or do we have to throw out large chunks of the Bible because it just isn't believable or applicable?

During this book we will spend some time in answering this question, and my prayer is that those reading this book with a sense of skepticism will be enlightened and find that God's Word is very much reliable.

6. The Problem of Boredom

"Zachary" is a Bible teacher in the Church. He approached the Pastor with a difficult problem. He said, "I really love to study the Bible. I love to learn the stories and how they apply to me.

The problem is that when I teach it, it seems that people are more interested in talking about how the Philadelphia Eagles clobbered the Pittsburg Steelers than the text. I'm not expecting people to become great theologians, but shouldn't people be more excited about God's Word? It just seems that they are bored with the Bible."

This is a huge issue that affects anyone who attempts to teach the Bible. It is very hard to get people excited about God's Word. I've noticed that for some, the Bible is boring until they find insights for their life situation. Suddenly, studying the Bible becomes a good investment of time.

Along this line of discussion, let me give you teachers a warning that guilt is a poor motivator. It's very powerful, but it is also poisonous. It kills the joy that should be in the life of the believer. Guilt eventually drives people away from the Scriptures, rather than into them.

How about You?
We've seen a number of reasons that people do not study the Bible. Take some time to evaluate the ones that applies to you.

- Do you question the Bible's relevance?
- Are you locked into a lack of process and technique?
- Do you lack basic skills?
- Are you convinced that the Bible is just for the professionals and it takes seminary training to really understand its meaning?

- Does the Bible carry such a low priority in your life?
- Do you perceive the Bible to be reliable?
- Do you view the Bible as boring?

If you identify with any of these reasons, then keep reading. Throughout this book I'm going to attempt to address each of these reasons. Remember that each one CAN be overcome.

Lesson 2

Why Study The Bible

As we have spent some time recognizing why we <u>don't</u> study the Bible as we should, let's also spend some time understanding why we <u>need</u> to study the Bible. I want you to see three benefits. But actually, they are not only benefits, they are essentials to your spiritual growth.

1. Bible Study Is Essential For Spiritual Growth

The Bible says, *"Like newborn babies, crave pure spiritual milk, so that by it you may grow up in your salvation"* (1 Peter 2:2). If you've ever been around a hungry baby, then you will understand the meaning of this passage. For, as a baby needs milk, so also, the young Christian should desire the pure milk of God's Word. Remember back when there was a baby in the house? Hunger drives a baby to weep and keep you up at night. But this food for babies is not just a delectable need.

They really desire it.

They crave it.

They love it.

Spiritual Milk are the simple aspects of the Christian faith, such as understanding the Gospel and being dependent on the Pastor or a teacher for your growth.

When our daughters were infants, we didn't just give them a little milk. If we did, we would put them in jeopardy to have stunted growth. Well, that's a great picture for a church that does not elevate God's Word. It puts that church in danger of stunted growth and maturity. We need to uplift God's Word in our spiritual lives. We need to see the necessity of it and want it, because we can't grow up without it.

2. The Study Of The Word Is Essential For Spiritual Maturity

Listen to what the author says in Hebrews 5. For in this passage the writer of Hebrews is telling us to start nourishing in the "solid food" of the Word of God. That is, go beyond the simple message of the Bible and begin getting into the depth of God's Word. Hebrews 5 says,

> *We have much to say about this, but it is hard to make it clear to you because you no longer try to understand.* [12] *In fact, though by this time you*

> *ought to be teachers, you need someone to teach you the elementary truths of God's word all over again. You need milk, not solid food! [13] Anyone who lives on milk, being still an infant, is not acquainted with the teaching about righteousness. [14] But solid food is for the mature who by constant use have trained themselves to distinguish good from evil*
>
> (Hebrews 5:11-14).

What this verse is saying is that we need "solid food" beyond the pure milk of God's Word. There comes a time in the life of a Christian when the simplicity of the milk of the Word just isn't enough to keep you nourished. So, are you satisfied with milk or do you desire the meat of God's Word?

3. The Study Of The Bible Is Essential For Spiritual Effectiveness

Two of the most important verses about the Bible come from 2 Timothy 3:16 and 17. They say, *"All Scripture is Inspired (God-breathed) and is useful for teaching, rebuking, correcting and training in righteousness, so that the man of God may be thoroughly equipped for every good work"* (2 Timothy 3:16-17).

I love that phrase. *"All Scripture"* is useful.

That includes every part of the Bible. It includes the least read books of the Old Testament, such as Numbers and Leviticus, as well as Habakkuk and Deuteronomy. Do you remember when Jesus was tempted three times in the desert by the devil, and each time what did He do? He quoted from where? He quoted from Deuteronomy. In fact, Deuteronomy 8 is Jesus' most quoted passage in the New Testament.

Imagine if your spiritual success this week was dependent on your knowledge of Deuteronomy and you never bothered with it? Only when we uphold the entire Word of God and not run away from complicated passages, will we truly become useful in God's hands.

I am guessing that all of us have, at some point in our spiritual journey, wondered or thought, "I would love to be more effective for God's Kingdom." The Word of God is the key to all of that!

It is essential for spiritual effectiveness if we are to grow in our walk in our spiritual journey.

Lesson 3

Who Can Study The Bible

Who can study the Bible? Are pastors and priests the only ones who can accurately study the Bible? Well, the good news is that anyone can study the Bible. Anyone on earth can study the Bible. But even though anyone can <u>study</u> the Bible, it seems that only those who have the Spirit of Christ can <u>understand</u> the Bible, and this is the key.

Let me give you some prerequisites to understanding the Word of God.

1. We Need To Be Saved In Order To Understand The Bible

Though many can read the Bible, the Scriptures say that only those who have put their faith in Christ can really understand the Bible. The reason is that at the moment of salvation, the Holy Spirit comes to live in you and He is the one who enables you to understand. 1 Corinthians 2:14-15 says, *"The person <u>without</u> the Spirit does not accept the things that come from the Spirit of God but considers them foolishness, and cannot understand them because they are discerned only through the Spirit. ¹⁵ The person <u>with</u> the Spirit makes judgments about all things, but such a person is not subject to merely human judgments."*

2. WE NEED THE SPIRIT OF GOD TO UNDERSTAND THE BIBLE

The Spirit has done a few things and does a few things with the Word. Please notice that there are a few key terms that are important for you to understand the work of the Spirit in the Bible:

- **The Holy Spirit <u>Inspired</u> The Word of God**

By saying that God *inspired* the Word of God, we are saying that God divinely influenced the human authors of the Scriptures in such a way that what they wrote was the very Word of God. In the context of the Scriptures, the word "inspiration" simply means "God-breathed." Inspiration means the Bible truly is the Word of God and makes the Bible unique among all other books.

There isn't any argument that the Bible itself claims that every word in every part of the Bible comes from God (1 Corinthians 2:12-13 and 2 Timothy 3:16-17). This view of Scripture is called "Verbal Plenary" inspiration.

- This means that it is "verbal" – the very words of God; not just concepts or ideas.

- It also means that it is "plenary" – which means that inspiration extends to all subject matters of Scripture. Hence "plenary"
- The two passages important to the concept of inspiration, are found in 2 Timothy 3, 2 Peter 1, as well as Matthew 5:17-18.

2 Timothy 3:16-17 says,

> *All Scripture is God-breathed and is useful for teaching, rebuking, correcting and training in righteousness, ¹⁷ so that the servant of God may be thoroughly equipped for every good work*
>
> (2 Timothy 3:16-17).

This verse tells us that God inspired *all* Scripture and that it is profitable to us. In other words, it is not just certain parts of the Bible which are inspired, but each and every word from Genesis to Revelation is inspired by God. The Bible then, is therefore authoritative when it comes to establishing doctrine, and sufficient for teaching man how be in a right relationship with God. The Bible claims not only to be inspired by God, but also to have the supernatural ability to change us and make us complete.

2 Peter 1:21 says,

> *For prophecy never had its origin in the human will, but prophets, though human, spoke from God as they were carried along by the Holy Spirit*
>
> (2 Peter 1:21).

This verse in 2 Peter helps us to understand that even though God used men with their distinctive personalities and writing styles, God divinely inspired the very words they wrote.

<u>Matthew 5:17-18 says,</u>
Jesus Himself confirmed the verbal plenary inspiration of the Scriptures when He said, *"Do not think that I have come to abolish the Law or the Prophets; I have not come to abolish them but to fulfill them. I tell you the truth, until heaven and earth disappear, not the smallest letter, not <u>the least stroke of a pen</u>, will by any means disappear from the Law..."* (Matthew 5:17-18).

Because the Scriptures are the inspired Word of God, we can have confidence that they are true and authoritative for life and godliness.

- **The Holy Spirit <u>Illumines</u> The Word Of God**

Bible teachers often use the word *<u>illumination</u>* to describe the work of the Holy Spirit that enables us to understand and apply the spiritual message of the Scriptures.

A wonderful example of what illumination entails comes to us from Luke 24 when Jesus met two disciples on the Emmaus Road. *" Then beginning with Moses and [throughout] all the [writings of the] prophets, He explained and interpreted for them the things referring to Himself [found] in all the Scriptures"* (Luke 24:27). Later, *"Then their eyes were [suddenly] opened [by God] and they [clearly] recognized Him; and He vanished from their sight"* (Luke 24:31). In illumination, the Holy Spirit opens our eyes so that we may know the Scriptures.

Illumination is a ministry of the Holy Spirit, Who is given *"that we might know the things that are freely given to us of God"* (1 Corinthians 2:12). When the Holy Spirit does this work in our life, it results in our gaining a fuller understanding of the Scriptures (John 16:13-15; 1 Corinthians 2:12-16).

The illuminating work of the Holy Spirit depends on our relationship with God. Sin can hinder our understanding of Scripture. Like David, we need to pray, *"Open my eyes that I may see wonderful things in your law"* (Psalms 119:18).

We cannot understand the Scriptures apart from the Holy Spirit's work of illumination. This is because our spiritual eyes are blinded so that we cannot see the things of God. The Bible speaks of the judicial blindness of Israel brought on by their rejection of Christ (Romans 11:25), the blindness of hatred (1 John 2:11), the blindness of Gentiles who had not yet been exposed to the light of the Gospel (Isaiah 9:2), the inability to see the kingdom of God apart from the new birth (John 3:3), and the work of Satan in blinding people to the Gospel today (2 Corinthians 4:3-4).

When the Holy Spirit illuminates the Scriptures, two things happen.

a) First, unsaved people are convicted of sin (John 16:8). The word "convict" is derived from a Latin expression meaning "cause to see."

b) Second, Christians gain a greater understanding of the Scriptures. Spiritual illumination is also called "the anointing of the Holy Spirit" (1 John 2:20, 27).

As you begin to study, the Holy Spirit illumines the Word of God and the Spirit of God is right there helping you to understand it; illuminating it and opening your eyes and your heart to see it.

- **The Holy Spirit <u>Instructs</u> And <u>Guides</u> Us Using The Word Of God**

There are five verses that talk about the Holy Spirit and His instruction or teaching us.

a) The Holy Spirit is a great reminder of God's Word to us.

> *But the Advocate, the Holy Spirit, whom the Father will send in my name, will teach you all things and will remind you of everything I have said to you*

> (JOHN 14:26).

b) The Holy Spirit teaches even in times of rebellion.

The context of Nehemiah 9:20 is that the nation of Israel is in rebellion and wandering in the wilderness, yet God was still actively working in their midst.

> *You gave your good Spirit to instruct them. You did not withhold your manna from their mouths, and you gave them water for their thirst*

> (NEHEMIAH 9:20).

c) The Holy Spirit in times when we need to defend our faith, will give us the words to say.

> *But when they arrest you, do not worry about what to say or how to say it. At that time you will be given what to say, [20] for it will not be you speaking, but the Spirit of your Father speaking through you*

(MATTHEW 10:19-20).

d) The Holy Spirit is able to provide the words even when facing persecution and death.

> *Whenever you are arrested and brought to trial, do not worry beforehand about what to say. Just say whatever is given you at the time, for it is not you speaking, but the Holy Spirit*

(MARK 13:11).

e) The Holy Spirit becomes your school teacher when you come to faith in Christ.

The phrase "the anointing you received" is past tense and refers to their salvation and the Holy Spirit's indwelling.

*As for you, the anointing you received from him
remain in you, and you do not need anyone
to teach you. But as his anointing teaches you
about all things and as that anointing is real,
not counterfeit—just as it has taught you,
remain in him*

(1 JOHN 2:27).

In summary, at the moment of your salvation, you have received Jesus as your Lord and Savior, and though the Holy Spirit has come to indwell your life and you have all of the Holy Spirit that you will ever need, the remaining question is, "Does the Holy Spirit have all of you?"

In Ephesians 5, Paul states, *"Do not be drunk with wine which leads to debauchery. Instead be filled with the Spirit"* (Ephesians 5:32). The "filling of the Spirit" is a deep desire to be instructed, examined and led by the Spirit and the Word of God. It is a constant sense of awareness that Christians cannot make on their own as believers and their need to be dependent on the Holy Spirit for guidance.

The Holy Spirit inspires the Word of God, then instructs and illumines the Word of God so that we can understand it and accept it.

Final Thoughts:

Many people have adopted a view where they are waiting for the Holy Spirit to speak, either verbally, in a vision, or through an "inner light." They read books by people who confidently say they are speaking on God's behalf. Emboldened, the reader may eagerly await, create, or fabricate a revelation from God. The desire to hear the Spirit speak is admirable. But the ironic truth is that the Spirit has already spoken. He has spoken in His Word.

If I expect direct revelation, who needs a Bible? I can simply ask God to speak, while I fail to study and absorb the vehicle through which He already has spoken. This shortcut or circumvention of direct revelation might be exciting, but it is a lazy man's approach, and a dangerous one. (I have many impulses and thoughts—how can I tell which are from God and which aren't?)

If I would listen to the voice of the Spirit, I should "put my ear" to the Word of God. Why wait for the Spirit to speak when I have in my hands what He has already spoken?

The distance between me and God's revelation is the distance between me and my Bible. I should prayerfully ask for the Holy Spirit's guidance in my biblical study, but not ask Him for new revelation independent of it.

Don't misunderstand. I believe that the Holy Spirit leads me and illuminates me every day. All I am saying is that I must weigh my subjective sense of what the Spirit is saying against the teachings of the Book that He inspired.

Lesson 4

Can Your Trust The 66 Books In Our Bible?

How can we be sure that we have the correct sixty-six books in our Bible? In reality the Bible has been translated into a number of languages, first in Latin, then English, and finally other languages. In fact, it is composed of sixty-six books by forty different writers over fifteen hundred years. But what makes it unique is that it has one consistent story with one ultimate author – God. The story is about God's plan to rescue humanity from the destructive results of the Fall; a plan that was conceived in eternity, revealed through the prophets, and carried out by the Son of God, Jesus Christ.[1]

Each writer of the Bible books wrote in his own language and style, using his own mind, and in some cases research, yet each was so overruled by the Holy Spirit that error was not allowed to creep into his work. For this reason, the Bible is understood by Christians to be a book without error.

This collection of sixty-six books is known as the canon of Scripture. The word comes from the Hebrew "Kanch" (a rod) and the Greek "Kanon" (a reed). The words refer equally to the measuring rod of a carpenter and ruler of a scribe. It became a common word for anything that was the measure by which others were to be judged (see Galatians 6:16, for example). After the Apostles, church leaders used it to refer to the body of Christian doctrine accepted by the churches. Clement and Origen of Alexandria, in the third century, were possibly the first to employ the word to refer to the Scriptures (the Old Testament).[2] From then on it became more common in Christian use as reference to a collection of books that are fixed in their number, divine in their origin, and universal in their authority.

In the earliest centuries there was little debate among Christians over which books belonged in the Bible; certainly by the time of the church leader Athanasius in the fourth century, the number of books had long been fixed. He set out the books of the New Testament just as we know them and added: "These are the springs of salvation that whoever thirsts may be satisfied by the expressiveness which is in them. In them is set forth the doctrine of devoutness. Let no one add to them."[3]

Today, there are a number of people who are trying to undermine the solid testimony of history. Dan Brown in the "Da Vinci

Code" stated, "More than eighty gospels were considered for the New Testament and yet only relatively few were chosen for inclusion."[4] Richard Dawkins, professor of Popular Science at Oxford, England, has made similar comments.[5]

So, what is the evidence for our collection of the sixty-six books? How certain can we be that these are the correct books to make up our Bible – no more and no less?

THE CANON OF THE OLD TESTAMENT

There really was no argument to the canon of the Old Testament. The Jews had a clearly defined body of Scriptures that was collectively agreed upon known as the Torah, or Law. This was secured early in the life of Israel and there was no doubt as to which books belonged and which did not.

- The Law was the first five books, known as the Pentateuch, which means "five rolls" – referring to the parchment scrolls on which they were normally written.
- The Prophets consisted of the Former Prophets (usually for us these included Joshua, Judges, Samuel, and Kings).
- The Latter Prophets consisted of Isaiah, Jeremiah, Lamentations, and the twelve smaller prophetic books.
- The Writings gathered up the rest. The total amounted generally to twenty-four books because many books, such as 1 and 2 Samuel, Ezra and Nehemiah, were counted as one.

When was the canon of the Old Testament settled? The simple response is that we accept each of the books as written at the time of its historical writing. <u>The first five books</u> were dated in the canon at the time of Moses. <u>The writings of David</u>, <u>the major and minor prophets</u> are also historically verifiable, therefore, they are also accepted in the canon immediately. So, then the successive stages of acceptance into the canon of Scripture is not hard to fix. Certainly, the Jews generally held this view.

There is a lot of internal evidence that the books of the Old Testament were written close to the time they record. For example, in 2 Chronicles 10:19, we have a record from the time of Rehoboam that "Israel has been in rebellion against the house of David until this day." Clearly, therefore that must have been recorded prior to 722 BC, when the Assyrians finally crushed Israel and the cream of the population was taken away into captivity – or at the very latest before 586 BC when Jerusalem suffered the same fate. We know also that the words of the prophets were written down in their own lifetime; Jeremiah had a secretary called Baruch for this very purpose (Jeremiah 36:4).

Josephus, the Jewish historian, clearly stated in his defense of Judaism that the Jews did not have many books. "For we have not an innumerable multitude of books among us and contradicting one another (as the Greeks have) but only twenty-two books, which contain the records of all the past times, which are justly believed to be divine."[6]

THE COUNCIL OF JAMNIA

Between AD 90 and 100, a group of Jewish scholars met at Jamnia in Israel to consider matters relating to the Hebrew Scriptures. It has been suggested that the canon of the Jewish Scriptures was agreed here; yet the reality is that there is no contemporary record of deliberations at Jamnia and our knowledge is therefore left to the comments of later rabbis.

The idea that there is <u>no clear canon</u> of the Hebrew Scriptures before AD 100 is not only in conflict with the testimony of Josephus and others, but has also been seriously challenged more recently. It is now generally accepted that Jamnia was not a council nor was the purpose of the meeting to be a ruling on the Jewish canon; rather it was an assembly that examined and discussed the Hebrew Scriptures.

The purpose of the council was not to decide which books should be included among the sacred writings, but to examine those that were already accepted.[7]

The Apocrypha And The Septuagint

There was a cluster of about 14 books known as the Apocrypha, which were written some time between the close of the Old Testament (after 400 BC) and the beginning of the New Testament. They were never considered as a part of the Hebrew Scriptures, and the Jews themselves clearly ruled them out by the confession that there was, throughout that period, no voice of the prophets in the land.[8] They looked forward to a day when "a faithful prophet" should appear."[9]

The Old Testament had been translated into Greek during the third century BC, and this translation is known as the Septuagint, a word meaning 70, after the seventy men involved in the translation work. It was the Greek Septuagint that the disciples of Jesus used, since Greek was the common language of the day.

Whether or not the Septuagint also contained the Apocrypha is impossible to say for certain, since although the earliest copies of the Septuagint available today do include the Apocrypha – placed at the end – these are dated in the fifth century and therefore cannot be relied upon to tell us what was common half a millennium earlier. Significantly, neither Jesus nor any of the apostles ever quoted from the Apocrypha, even though they were obviously using the Greek Septuagint. Josephus was familiar with the Septuagint and made use of it, but he never considered the Apocrypha part of the Scriptures.[10]

The Dead Sea Scrolls

The collection of scrolls that has become available since the discovery of the first texts in 1947 near Wadi Qumran, close by the Dead Sea, does not provide scholars with a definitive list of Old Testament books. Even if it did, it would not necessarily tells us what mainstream orthodox Judaism believed. After all, the Samaritans used only their own version of the Pentateuch, but they did not represent mainstream Judaism.

What can be said for certain, however, is that Old Testament books are represented among the Qumran collection with the exception of Esther and they are quoted frequently as Scripture. Nothing else, certainly not the Apocrypha, is given the same status.

In spite of suggestions by critical scholars to the contrary, there is no evidence, not even from the Dead Sea Scrolls, that there were other books contending for a place within the Old Testament canon.

For the Jews, therefore, Scripture as a revelation from God through the prophets ended around 450 BC with the close of the book of Malachi. This was the Bible of Jesus and His disciples, and it was precisely the same in content as our Old Testament.

The New Testament scholar John Wenham concludes: "There is no reason to doubt that the canon of the Old Testament is substantially Ezra's canon, just as the Pentateuch was substantially Moses' canon."[11]

TRANSITION: JESUS AND HIS DISCIPLES

The Christian community, both in the days of Jesus and in centuries following had no doubt that there was a body of books that made up the records of the old covenant. There are literally hundreds of direct quotations or clear allusions to the Old Testament passages. It is important to take note that the Apocrypha is never quoted by the New Testament writers.

While it is true that some of the early church leaders quoted from the Apocrypha, though very rarely, there is no evidence that they recognized these books as equal to the authority of the Old Testament.[12]

THE CANON OF THE NEW TESTAMENT

The earliest available list of the New Testament books is known as the Muratorian Canon and is dated around 150 AD. It includes the four gospels, the thirteen Pauline epistles, three letters of John, and the Revelation of John. It claims that these were accepted by the "universal Church." This leaves out 1 and 2 Peter, James and Hebrews.

However, 1 Peter was widely accepted by this time and might be an oversight by the compiler (or the copyist). By AD 240, Origen from Alexandria was using all 27 books as "Scripture" and no others, and referred to them as the "New Testament."[13] He believed them to be "inspired by the Spirit."[14] But it was not until AD 367 that Athanasius, also from Alexandria, provided us with an actual list of New Testament books identical with ours.[15]

However, long before we had that list, the evidence shows that 27 books, and only those, were widely accepted as Scripture.

Why Did It Take That Long?

The New Testament was not all neatly printed and bound by the Israeli Publishing Press Company in Philippi and sent out to all the bookstores after Paul's death. Here are six reasons why it took time for the books of the New Testament to be gathered together.

The originals were scattered throughout the entire Roman Empire. The Roman Empire spanned from Britain to Persia and it would have taken a long time for the letters to be collected.

No scroll could easily contain more than one or two books. It would be impossible to fit more than one Gospel into a scroll, and even when books were used, the entire New Testament would be extremely bulky and very expensive to produce.

The first century Christians expected the immediate return of Christ. Because of this, they didn't plan for the long-term future of the Church.

No one church or leader bossed all the others. There were strong leaders and respected leaders in the church, but there weren't supreme bishops who dictated to all the others which books belonged to the canon and which did not.

The early leaders assumed the authority of the Gospels and the Apostles. It was considered sufficient to quote the Gospels and Apostles, since the authority was self-evident.

Only when the heretics attacked the truth was the importance of a canon appreciated. It was not until the mid-second century that the Gnostics and others began writing their false teachings which prompted the orthodox leaders to become aware of the need for stating which books should be recognized as the canon across the Church.

What Made A Book A Scripture?

The churches felt no need to describe which books were special and should be made in equal footing with the Old Testament Scriptures, because if the letter came from one of the apostles, that was adequate. But, through time, others began to submit letters and gospels and propagate their own ideas. Therefore, five tests were developed and necessary to discern truth from error.

1. Apostolic test – Does It Come From An Apostle?

The first Christians asked, "Was it written by an Apostle or under the direction of an Apostle?" This was in line with the Old Testament where the Jews had expected that the Old Testament Scriptures would be written by prophets.

2. Genuine – Does It Sound As Truthful?

In 1 Thessalonians 2:13 it says, "And we also thank God continually because, when you received the word of God, which you heard from us, you accepted it not as a human word, but as it actually is, the word of God, which is indeed at work in you who believe." There was this authoritative undertone to the message.

3. Ancient – Has It Been Used From The Earliest Times?

Most of the false writings were rejected simply because they were too new to be Apostolic. Early in the fourth century, Athanasius listed the New Testament canon as we know it today and claimed that these were the books "received by us through tradition as belonging to the Canon."[16]

4. Circulated Among Churches – Are Most Of The Churches Using It?

It took time for many of the epistles to circulate among the churches. It is all the more significant that 23 or 27 books were almost universally accepted well before the middle of the second century. That is pretty early in church history for the canon to be almost completed.

5. ACCURATE – DOES IT CONFORM TO THE HISTORICAL TEACHING OF THE CHURCH?

There was an extensive settlement among the churches across the empire as to the content of the Christian message. Irenaeus asked the question whether a particular writing was consistent with what the church taught.[17] This is what ruled out so much of the heretical material immediately.

6. FORESIGHT BY GOD – IT IS GOD-BREATHED.

The final appeal is not to man, nor to the early church leaders, but to God, who by His Holy Spirit has put His seal upon the New Testament. By their spiritual content and by the claim of their human writers, the 27 books of our New Testament form part of the "God breathed" Scripture. It is perfectly correct to allow this divine intervention to guard the process by which eventually all the canonical books, and no others, were accepted. The idea of the final canon being an accident and that any number of books could have ended up in the Bible, ignores the evident unity and provable accuracy of the whole collection of 27 books.

Bruce Metzger expressed it well: "There are, in fact, no historical data that prevent one from acquiescing in the conviction held by the Church Universal that, despite the very human factors…in the production, preservation, and collection of the books of the New Testament, the whole process can also be rightly characterized as the result of divine overruling."[18]

Authority Of Scriptures = 66 Canon

If you believe in the authority of the Scriptures, then you have to believe in the divine preservation of the canon. The two are inseparable.

For the God who "breathed out" (2 Timothy 3:16) His Word into the minds of the writers, ensured that those books, and no others, formed part of the completed canon of the Bible.

To tear out major portions of it, because of cultural changes or moral rejections is to reject God's breath. A great warning is given at the end of the book of Revelation that anyone who dares to tear out a portion of God's Word must heed:

> *I warn everyone who hears the words of the prophecy of this scroll: If anyone adds anything to them, God will add to that person the plagues described in this scroll. ¹⁹ And if anyone takes words away from this scroll of prophecy, God will take away from that person any share in the tree of life and in the Holy City, which are described in this scroll.*
>
> Revelation 22:18-19

[1] Brian Edwards, *Nothing But the Truth*, (Darlington, UK, Evangelical Press, 2006) pgs 116-143).

[2] Clement of Alexandria. The Miscellanies bk. Vol. 15. He comments, "The ecclesiastical rule (canon) is the concord and harmony of the Law and the Prophets." B.F Westcott, referring to *Origen's Commentary on Matthew* 28, wrote, "No one should use for proof of doctrine books not included among the canonized Scriptures." (*The Canon of the New Testament During the First Four Centuries* (Cambridge: Macmillan & Co. 1855), p 548.

[3] *Fiestal Epistle of Athanasius XXXIX*. Translated in Nicene and Post-Nicene Fathers, Volume IV pages 551-552.

[4] Dan Brown, *The Da Vinci Code* (London: Bantam Press, 2003), page 231.

[5] Richard Dawkins, *The God Delusion* (London: Bantam Press, 2006), page 237.

[6] Josephus, *Against Apion*, translated William Whiston (London: Ward Lock & Co.,) book 1, chapter 8.

[7] This is a widespread view. See for example: R. Beckwith. *The Old Testament Canon of the New Testament Church* (London: SPCK, 1985), page 275. Also, Bruce Metzger, *The Canon of the New Testament* (Oxford: Oxford University Press, 1987) page 110.

[8] *The Apocrypha*. 1 Maccabees 9:27 at the time of revolt against Syrian occupation in the mid second century BC by Judas Maccabeas, "*There was a great affliction in Israel, the like whereof was not since the time that a prophet was not seen among them.*"

[9] *The Apocrypha*. 1 Maccabees 14:41.

[10] It should be noted that the Roman Catholic and Eastern Orthodox Churches do accept some of the Apocryphal books as Scripture because they support, for example the praying for the dead.

[11] John Wenham. *Christ and the Bible* (London: Tyndale Press, 1972) page 134.

[12] This is a point made firmly by John Wenham in *Christ And the Bible* pages 146-147.

[13] Origen. *De Principlis* (Concerning Principles), pref. 4. He used the title "New Testament" six times in *De Principlis*.

[14] Origen. *De Principlis*, Pref. 4, Ch. 3:1.

[15] From the *Fiestal Epistle of Athanasius XXXIX*. Translated in Nicene and Post-Nicene Fathers, Vol. IV. Pages 551-552. This is what he wrote: "As the heretics are quoting apocryphal writings, an evil which was rife even as early as when St. Luke wrote his gospel, therefore I have through good to set forth clearly what books have been received by us through tradition as belonging to the Canon, and which we believe to be divine. (Then follows the books of the Old Testament with the unusual addition of the book of *Baruch*). Of the New Testament books …then follows the 27 books of the New Testament and no more. These are the fountains of salvation, that whoever thirsts may be satisfied, which is in them. In them alone is set forth the doctrine of piety. Let no one add to them, nor take anything from them."

[16] Athanasius. *Fiesta Epistle XXXIX*.

[17] Irenaeus. *Against Heresies*. Book III. Chapter 3.3

[18] Metzger. *The Canon of the New Testament*. Page 286.

Lesson 5

Is The Bible Really Necessary To Know God

When I was a teenager I went camping with my friends from church quite often. Growing up in the city of Philadelphia seeing stars at night was a major treat. Yes, we saw stars in Philadelphia. But when you get out away from the city lights, you really are overwhelmed by the feeling of awe and wonder from the night sky. You get a feeling of the vastness of God's creation.

Let me ask you: when you are in the midst of nature such as in a forest, or by the sea, or on a mountain peak, do you ever feel a sense of the sacred, like the feeling in a vast cathedral? Sadly, I went onto a pantheist website where they argued that there is no personal God outside the universe, but that nature itself is sacred and to revered. [1]

There is some truth in the experience of our pantheist friends. Nature should fill us with feelings of awe and wonder. We should feel like worshipping when we walk through a beautiful forest or stand by the awesome sea. Rather than make us skeptical about God, nature should cause us to recognize that there is someone greater than ourselves. The glory of the universe points us to the glory of the One who made it. "Holy, holy, holy is the Lord of hosts; the whole earth is full of His glory!" (Isaiah 6:3).

SOME THINGS THAT WE CAN KNOW WITHOUT THE BIBLE

First, the Bible is not necessary for us to know that there is a God. It is not necessary to intuitively know that we have broken His rules and are deserving of His punishment. God has revealed Himself through His creation and our consciences. Romans 1 says: *"For since the creation of the world God's invisible qualities—his eternal power and divine nature—have been clearly seen, being understood from what has been made, so that people are without excuse"* (Romans 1:20). Romans 2, then expands that thought, *"They show that the requirements of the law are written on their hearts, their consciences also bearing witness, and their thoughts sometimes accusing them and at other times even defending them"* (Romans 2:15). Rational minds can understand that behind the beauty and power of the universe is a God who created it, and that they, therefore, are responsible to their Creator.

But because we live in a fallen world, this knowledge about God and His ways is always imperfect and can be mistaken. Sin warps our minds so we become futile in our thinking, foolishness plunging our hearts into darkness.[2] Ephesians squarely places responsibility of not knowing God on the hardened hearts of humankind: *"They are darkened in their understanding and separated from the life of God because of the ignorance that is in them due to the hardening of their hearts"* (Ephesians 4:18). Louis Berkhof, an early twentieth-century theologian, wrote about the consequences of sin: "God's handwriting in nature was obscured and corrupted, and man was stricken with spiritual blindness, became subject to error and unbelief, and now in his blindness and perverseness fails to read aright even the remaining traces of the original revelation, and is unable to understand any further revelation of God.[3] Due to the corruption of sin, we need the Bible to correctly interpret creation. We need it to interpret our own consciences.

Grab A Chair –The Bible Is Necessary

We need the Bible in order to really know God. You know Dr. David Jeremiah, Andy Stanley, and Francis Chan. You may have heard a sermon or two from one of these top guys. You may even have read an article about them or followed them on their blogs. But I really doubt you know them intimately. You can know a famous person, but it would be a different kind of knowing if he pulled up a chair next to you and told you all about himself and his ultimate goals in his life. If he spent time with you and shared about his family and his fears and successes. We cannot truly know a person unless we spend time with them. I mean, a lot of time, to get to know them intimately.

The same is more so about our transcended God. He cannot be known unless He makes Himself known. Thankfully, in His graciousness, God has chosen to disclose Himself to sinful undeserving people. He revealed Himself in the Bible.

That is, the doctrine of the necessity of the Bible means the Bible is necessary for salvation, to grow as a Christian, and to know how to live out God's will in our lives, individually and corporately. We need the Bible to know God in a personal way. I don't mean that one must be literate or have a copy of the Bible. One can be told the message of the Gospel and taught what the Scriptures say. But without the message of the Bible, one cannot know God personally.

Bible Anorexia Versus Healthy Doses Of The Word Of God

The Christian life starts with the Bible and grows by the Bible. Just as we need food to feed our bodies, we need the Bible to feed our souls. Jesus said, "It is written: *'Man shall not live on bread alone, but on every word that comes from the mouth of God"* (Matthew 4:4). Our bodies require bread each day to survive. Our souls require regular meals from the Scriptures or they starve. And notice the "every" in Matthew 4:4. We need all of God's Word to keep us healthy, not just verses here and there. A. W. Tozer said, "*Nothing less than a whole Bible can make a whole Christian.*"

I had a friend who had anorexia nervosa. Anorexia is a disease that ravages some women. It causes weight loss from a refusal to eat. This leads to abnormal blood counts, fatigue, thinning hair, irregular heart rhythms and low blood pressure. The severe malnourishment caused by anorexia can result in damage to the brain, heart and kidneys. The scary thing is that girls and women with anorexia can't see how thin they are. When they look in the mirror, they don't notice bones protruding. In fact, they may even think they see fat.

Christians can have Bible anorexia. I remember a woman from a neighborhood Bible study sharing with me that she loved going there because they would open the Bible (and at that point she opened her Bible) and then she would get to go home and shut the Bible until next week's study.

This woman was a busy mom who served in the nursery at her church, sang in the worship team and at times helped in the children's ministry, but she did not realize she needed the "regular" and "personal" spiritual nourishment of God's Word at home. To her, Bibles were for church meetings. Interestingly, she was unhappy in life and was thinning out spiritually, even in the midst of all her serving. She had Bible anorexia.

SPIRITUAL FOOD

God has graciously given us His Word to keep us alive and spur us on to grow. 2 Peter 1:3-4 says, **"His divine power has given us everything we need for a godly life through our knowledge of him who called us by his own glory and goodness. *4 Through these he has given us his very great and precious promises, so that through them you may participate in the divine nature, having escaped the corruption in the world caused by evil desires."** Please notice that God's divine power works through the knowledge of Christ. Through the grace of God, we come to know Christ and gain eternal life. Through the grace of God, we grow in godliness as our knowledge of Christ increases. Through the precious and great promises of God's Word, we escape the corruption of the world and become partakers of the divine nature. At the end of his letter, Peter exhorts his readers, "*But grow in the grace and knowledge of our Lord and Savior Jesus Christ. To him be glory both now and forever! Amen.*"

Paul also repeatedly exhorts his readers to grow in their knowledge of Christ. In his letters, he teaches about Christ, encourages others to teach about Christ, and urges all to hold fast to the teachings about Christ.[4] He prays in Philippians 1:9-11, "*...that your love may abound more and more in knowledge and depth of insight, [10] so that you may be able to discern what is best and may be pure and blameless for the day of Christ, [11] filled with the fruit of righteousness that comes through Jesus Christ—to the glory and praise of God.*" In the modern world we think of love as simply a feeling, but God even wants our love to abound in knowledge. This means that we can't know how to love God and others well unless God teaches us. Our love grows and deepens as we know God better and receive instruction from His Word on how to love God. As our knowledge and discernment grow, we are purified and bear fruit that rebounds to the glory of God.

The Sword Of The Spirit Is The Word Of God

If we live by the Spirit, we will bear the fruit of the Spirit: "love, joy, peace, patience, kindness, goodness, faithfulness, gentleness, self-control" (Galatians 5:22-23). How do we live by the

Spirit? Romans 8 describes a war between the flesh and the Spirit. Living by the Spirit is a struggle against the idols of this world that tempt us every day. It is a pitched battled against the evil and out of control desires of our hearts. What will my affections be centered on today? What will my heart go after? What do I want more than anything else? Comfort? Reputation? Something to satisfy the senses? To do battle, we set out minds on the Spirit (Romans 8:5) and "put to death the misdeeds of the body," (Romans 8:13) by the Spirit, which is the "Word of God" (Ephesians 6:17). With the Word of God, we nourish the roots of our hearts and grow the sweet fruit of the Spirit. Without God's Word those roots shrivel and die.

The Word Of God Builds Up Strength For Those Weaker Days In Our Lives

Our lives are not static. We are moving in one direction or the other. Our physical bodies are all moving closer to the end. No matter what or how much we eat, our bodies eventually break down and waste away. But spiritual food can build up our souls day by day.

This gives us great hope, even as we age and go through various trials. This means that the investment in God's daily devotions today, will reap a dividend in the future. 2 Corinthians 4:16-18 says, *"Therefore we do not lose heart. Though outwardly we are wasting away, yet inwardly we are being renewed day by day. [17] For our light and momentary troubles are achieving for us an eternal glory that far outweighs them all. ¹⁸ So we fix our eyes not on what is seen, but on what is unseen, since what is seen is temporary, but what is unseen is eternal."* How do we look to the unseen, the eternal things? We open our Bibles and read. We meditate on the Scriptures. We ingest healthy doses of the Word of God EACH DAY. As we think on Christ and the Bible, eternity is opened up to us. Heavenly lights grow brighter while the worldly sparks dim. Our souls are renewed and prepared for that day when our weak eyes will be strengthened to behold the beams of indescribable glory that we reflect back to our magnificent Creator.

THE CHURCH LEADERSHIP'S NEED TO DIG INTO GOD'S WORD

Just as individuals need the Bible to know and follow God's Word and His will, churches need the Bible to rightly function according to God's will. In Ephesians, Paul describes the church as the household of God, a holy temple: *"Consequently, you are no longer foreigners and strangers, but fellow citizens with God's people and also members of his household, ²⁰ built on the foundation of the apostles and prophets, with Christ Jesus himself as the chief cornerstone. ²¹ In him the whole building is joined together and rises to become a holy temple in the Lord"* (Ephesians 2:19-21).[5] The foundation of this dwelling place for God is the apostles and prophets, the people who proclaimed the Word of God, which is encompassed in the Scriptures. A church that is not focused on the Bible is a house without a foundation.

CHURCHES TRADE THE WORD OF GOD FOR CULTURAL ADAPTATION

It's a tragedy when the God-breathed Scripture written to local churches by the founders of the universal church is seen as no longer needed by the church. These documents come from the Head of the church (the Lord), explain how to organize the church and are authoritative for the church, but inexplicably some churches have decided they no longer need them for more than an occasional consultation and have traded them in for *"cultural adaptation."*

J. I. Packer was asked for advice to church leaders. He said, *"Dig deep and dwell deep. I think that superficiality is the great weakness of the evangelical world today. I don't think that the skill in dramatic entertainment, which so many evangelical leaders are past masters in, makes up in any way for the failure to dig deep and dwell deep in the realities of Scripture truth and Scripture life."*[6] The church cannot function rightly without its leaders digging and dwelling deep in the Scriptures and encouraging their congregants to do the same. Churches should read, sing and preach the Word of God. Otherwise they become empty and shallow, like fancy entertainment centers without any substance to fill them.

AN APPEAL TO PERSONAL STUDY OF GOD'S WORD

My appeal to Sunday School teachers, Small Group leaders and Bible Study facilitators is to begin to move away from the video series co-dependency that our era is being known for. We have become somewhat lazy (present company accepted) by popping in a DVD five minutes prior to a Small Group meeting, and then asking the "proverbial" question "So, what do you think?"

No preparation necessary!
No Bible study needed!
No personal interaction with God's Word!
No personal application!

And at the same time, we feel we get the credit for being good Small Group leaders. Friends, I am not saying that we should abandon videos or video series. There are a number of great topics that have the depth that we could never obtain on our own. But somehow, we have become "lazy" and have literally advocated "Bible Study" to a minimal role in the local church. Let's reverse that trend.

If not knowing how to study God's Word is the problem, then the next section of this book will provide some valuable tools for you to use. As always, it comes down to practicing these three steps. These steps are not unique to me. They have been taught to pastors for centuries. We'll be looking at the: (1) Observation; (2) Interpretation; and (3) Application.

A Feast For Your Souls

My hope and prayer is that you will find in God's Word a feast for your souls. Because human beings are finite, we can never know God fully or exhaustively; however, we can know Him truly and substantially through His Word. Salvation, growth, and knowledge of God's will are an offer in the Bible. Christians and their churches must fill themselves with the Scriptures. Starving ourselves makes us weak. The Bible sustains us and makes us healthy.

J.C. Ryle, the author of *Holiness*, asked, "What is the cause of your weakness? Is it not because the fountain of life is little used? Is it not because you are resting on old experiences, and not daily gathering new manna – daily drawing new strength from Christ?"[7] He would urge us, "Gather your manna fresh every morning."[8]

When you look at the stars and moon at night are you overwhelmed by their beauty? When you visit a forest with the grand trees and towering mountain peaks are you taken aback by its splendor? Their beauty is nothing compared to the magnificence of Christ. You are only getting a partial picture. For through the Scriptures, Christ awaits to give for you a feast for your souls!

[1] Pantheism.net. *"Are you a Scientific Pantheist?"* Paul Harrison.
[2] Romans 1:21
[3] Louis Berkhof, *"A Summary of Christian Doctrine"* (Edinburgh, UK: Banner of Truth Trust, 2005), page 6.
[4] Second Thessalonians 2:15.
[5] See also Revelation 21:12-14.
[6] "J.I. Packer: Interview" by Carl Trueman, May 18, 2012.
[7] "J.C. Ryle, Living or Dead?" https://www.the-highway.com/living-or-dead_Ryle.html.
[8] "J.C. Ryle, Eight Profitable Ways To Read The Bible." http://www.ourmanna.com/articles/basic-bible/8-profitable-ways-to-read-the-bible/

Lesson 6

Today - Is The Bible Enough For Us?

Some say that the Bible is irrelevant. Times have changed! The internet has taken over to the extent that we can have constant access to and are in constant need of entertainment. We live, not bound to a provincial village or town, but in a world where media and culture have gone global. In this modern world, is the Bible still relevant? Has God's Word gone stale? Don't we need something more to add to give the Bible some color?

Recently, I went into a secular bookstore and found a popular author who took the words of Jesus and passed them onto her readers so that they "can experience them" directly. Other books uncovered the "secrets" from God. And of course, there are a myriad of books describing the first person accounts of heaven from people who claim to have been there and back.

Do we really need to tell such tales about Jesus and heaven and God's purposes for our lives? Do we really need a "fresh" account from God in order to make the Bible "real?" No! Our great God who knows the end from the beginning has already spoken and continues to speak through His Word today. We don't need to subtract from His words to appeal to people with post-modern views. Happily, we can apply the Bible to our complicated, global lives today and everyday. The Bible has been and always will be sufficient. Take it from a young boy who claimed to go to heaven and came back, and then retracted his statement: "I said I went to heaven because I thought it would it get me attention. When I made the claims that I did, I had never read the Bible. People have profited from lies, and continue to. They should read the Bible, which is enough. The Bible is the only source of truth."[1]

The Doctrine Of Sufficiency

The doctrine of sufficiency of Scripture means that the Scriptures contain every word we need for knowing the way of salvation and for living a godly life. This means that we don't need to know anything about God that is not contained in the Bible. It means that from the beginning of our spiritual lives to the end of our earthly lives we don't need any knowledge outside of the Bible about how to live and please God. No other knowledge is needed for Christian life and doctrine. The Bible alone is sufficient for these things. As the boy who didn't go to heaven said, the Bible is enough.

No New Revelation To The Bible

It is finished. We don't need any new, nor should we expect any new revelation from God. Hebrews 1:1-3 says: *"In the past God spoke to our ancestors through the prophets at many times and in various ways, ² but in these last days he has spoken to us by his Son, whom he appointed heir of all things, and through whom also he made the universe. ³ The Son is the radiance of God's glory and the exact representation of his being, sustaining all things by his powerful word. After he had provided purification for sins, he sat down at the right hand of the Majesty in heaven."*

God spoke "at many times and various ways" through Old Testament prophets. After setting the stage of redemptive history, God sent His Son, the exact representation of His being, as His final revelation. When Jesus completed His work making purification for sins, He finally revealed God. And so He sat down at the right hand of His Father. His work was done. God has now spoken to us by His Son.

No Adding Or Subtracting

Since God's Word is complete, we must not add to or subtract from it.[2] Jesus would commonly rail against the Pharisees for adding to the Word of God. In Mark 7:9 He said, *You have a fine way of setting aside the commands of God in order to observe your own traditions!"* The Pharisees required the Jews to ritually wash their hands, utensils, and even their dining furniture before meals and criticized Jesus' disciples for not following those rules. Yet, their hearts were not clean. Jesus confronted the Pharisees for subtracting from the Scripture, by allowing men to dedicate money to God that had originally been set aside to care for aging parents. The command to "Honor your father and your mother," was made void in the name of their devotion to God (Mark 7:13).

Two Common Examples Of Adding And Subtraction

To illustrate the addition to Scripture: I read this story where a man was in an accident and injured his back. While attending a church service an older woman came over to him and asked if she could anoint him with oil and pray over him. Appreciating all prayer, he had no objections. She gathered some friends around him, but what followed was a shock! After a short prayer, the woman asked the man when he had stopped reading horoscopes? She had received a "word from the Lord" that it was the reason why he was hurting. If he would confess, the pain would go away. This man insisted he was never into horoscopes, but the woman became even more vocal. Elevating fallible impressions to the level of God speaking can be not only presumptuous, but also hurtful and devastating.

To illustrate the deletion of Scripture: a young couple recently expressed doubts about the church's statement of faith because we believe in marriage between a man and a woman. We also do not believe that couples should live together prior to being married. This couple had decided to live together. They were believers and up to this point believed in the Bible, but now they had to pick and choose what portions they would accept.

There's nothing wrong with tradition or subjective experience. Traditions and experiences can be helpful in the Christian life, but they are poor substitutes for the rock-solid truth of the Scriptures. The Bible is God speaking. Statements of faith, creeds, orders of services, experiences and impressions are all useful to the extent that they are found in God's Word, but they should never replace Scripture.

THE SUFFICIENCY OF SCRIPTURE

Let me end this section with proclaiming the sufficiency of Scripture in 2 Timothy 3:16-17. It says this: *"All Scripture is God-breathed and is useful for teaching, rebuking, correcting and training in righteousness, [17] so that the servant of God may be thoroughly equipped for every good work."*

1. THE BIBLE IS PROFITABLE FOR TEACHING

It teaches us about a good God and our rebellion against Him. It teaches about God's Son, Jesus and the atonement He made for the sins of His people. It teaches us about the eternal life we can have as a result of the work Jesus has done. Scripture teaches us about singleness, marriage, work and family. There is nothing we need to know about God, His creation, and His Kingdom that the Bible does not teach us.

2. THE BIBLE IS PROFITABLE FOR REPROOF

We see our sin in the Scriptures. When a doctor performs surgery, he usually has to cut through bone or cartilage. It leaves a lot of damage before things are set in place and healing can occur. In the same fashion, Hebrews 4:12-13 describes God's Word as sharp enough to cut through the bone. *"For the word of God is alive and active. Sharper than any double-edged sword, it penetrates even to dividing soul and spirit, joints and marrow; it judges the thoughts and attitudes of the heart. [13] Nothing in all creation is hidden from God's sight. Everything is uncovered and laid bare before the eyes of him to whom we must give account"* (Hebrews 4:12-13). In a heart surgery, the heart is laid out and exposed before the surgeon, and so are our hearts laid out before God when we open God's Word. The sharp Word is thrust into our thoughts and intentions. The prophet Jeremiah warns that *"The heart is deceitful above all things, and beyond cure. Who can understand it?"* (Jeremiah 17:9). Surgery is often what our sick heart needs.

3. THE BIBLE IS PROFITABLE FOR CORRECTION

The Scripture doesn't just point to our sin, it turns us to the right direction. Just as the goal of the surgeon is to heal the patient, God's Word doesn't leave us in despair. Romans 5 says, *"For if, while we were God's enemies, we were reconciled to him through the death of his Son, how much more, having been reconciled, shall we be saved through his life! [11] Not only is this so, but we also boast in God through our Lord Jesus Christ, through whom we have now received reconciliation* (Romans 5:10-11).

4. The Bible Is Profitable For Training In Righteousness

As we regularly take time in the Word of God, our lives are molded like Christ. Just as tea infuses a pot of water with rich flavor, the Word of God transforms us. When we delight in God's Word and meditate on it day and night, we are like trees planted by streams of water that grow healthy leaves and yield fruit in season (Psalm 1:2-3). The tree in Psalm 1 is a God-breathed picture of righteousness as we exercise our minds, soaking up God's Word.

As God teaches us, reproves us, corrects us and trains us by His written Word, we become competent – ready, willing and able for every good work. We come to know God better, turn from sin, obey, make wise decisions and persevere in trials through the work of God's Word in us.

Hear The Voice Of God

The Bible is enough. The Scriptures contain every word we need for knowing the way of salvation and living a God-glorifying life.

C.H. Spurgeon suffered from chronic pain and ill health. His wife was an invalid, and to make matters worse, he was routinely criticized and attacked. He said, *"Believer! There is enough in the Bible for you to live on forever. If you should outnumber the years of Methuselah, there would be no need for a fresh revelation; if you should live until Christ returns, there would be no necessity for the addition of one single word; if you should go down as deep as Jonah, or even descend as David said he did, into the depths of hell, still there would be enough in the Bible to comfort you without one extra sentence.*[3]

Spurgeon knew that all that the believer needs is the Bible. We don't need a more personal message to feel closer to Jesus. He speaks directly to us through His Word. We don't need secrets uncovered; God has revealed Himself in the Bible. God has given us everything we need in the Scriptures to know how to think and live in ways that please Him and give us joy. Nothing can be added and no writings rival the Scriptures. We can be content with what God has told us in the Bible.

Do you need direction in life? Are you searching for true joy? Don't struggle through life wondering what God is saying or doing, while your Bible sits closed on your shelf.

Pull it out!

Open it up and hear the very voice of God as He speaks to you!

[1] Washington Post, "Boy Who Came Back From Heaven Actually Didn't; Books Recalled" by Ron Charles, (January 16, 2015).

[2] Deuteronomy 4:2; Proverbs 30:5-6; 1 Corinthians 4:6; Revelation 22:18-19

[3] C.H. Spurgeon, "Spurgeon's Gems" #93, http://www.biblebb.com//files/spurgeon/csg-051-100.htm

Part 2

Three Steps To Studying The Bible

If I were the Devil, one of my first aims would be to stop folks from digging into the Bible. I should do all I could to surround it with the spiritual equivalent of pits, thorns, hedges and mantraps to frighten people off.

J.I. Packer

The last twenty years I have seen a renewal of interest in the Scriptures. I have seen in my own church a greater desire for Bible studies, whether they come in the form of personal or group study. At the same time, Bible study tools in the form of videos and Internet teaching have also become readily available. Place that alongside of the Bible study leaders' lack of time to prepare and you have a perfect storm for non-preparation in God's Word.

This is not just a difficulty for Small Group, Sunday School, and Bible teachers. Busy pastors can also face the tyranny of the urgency. And that's why we all need to see the need to dig into the Scriptures individually and "own" the Word of God as we impart the Word to those we teach.

We need to stop becoming so co-dependent on others, and begin to depend on the Holy Spirit to illuminate our eyes with His Word.

- We need to stop "googling" for quick Biblical answers.
- We need to stop becoming so dependent on DVD teaching series and YouTube videos for providing sustenance for our churches.

We need to re-learn the three steps to studying the Bible. We need to learn (1) Observation; (2) Interpretation; and (3) Application. This section of the book will be more practical, then anything else. So, at the end of each section, I want to give you an opportunity to practice on a passage of Scripture.

Lesson 7

Step One - Observation

Observation teaches you to see what the passage says and is the basis for accurate interpretation and correct application. It is vitally important to understand the context of the Scripture being studied and not to pull the words or sentences away from their true meaning. Observation answers the question, "What does the passage say?"

You don't have to earn a degree in Greek, Hebrew, and Aramaic to figure out the correct context of any portion of Scripture. But it's essential that you keep in mind that language changes over time, and that speech patterns, writing styles, and communication methods differ during the course of our own lifetime, much less over 2,000 years. The observation techniques that follow allow you to glean what is being said in the proper context as you study.

Begin With Prayer

If you want to hear what God has to say to you personally, you really need to enter into 2-way communication. Prayer begins the conversation and places your mind, heart and soul in the right relationship with Him.

Ask The 5 W's And An H

The hardest thing to do is ridding ourselves of assumptions when we approach God's Word, whether it's a familiar or an unfamiliar passage. Presuppositions are the most common culprits leading to wrong interpretation and misapplication. Carefully observing who, what, when, where, why and how are the best assurances leading to correct interpretation. DON'T RUSH PAST THIS. Doing this on a chapter-by-chapter basis consistently places the paragraphs, sentences, and words in their proper context. The five W's and the one H are as follows:

- WHO is speaking? Who is this about? Who are the main characters? To whom is he speaking?
- WHAT is the subject or event covered in the chapter? What do you learn about the people, event, or teaching?
- WHEN do/will the events occur or did/will something happen to someone in particular?
- WHERE did or will this happen? Where was it said?
- WHY is something being said or mentioned? Why would/will this happen? Why at that time and/or to this person/people?
- HOW will it happen? How is it to be done? How is it illustrated?

MARK KEY WORDS AND PHRASES

A key word or phrase is one which, when removed, leaves the passage void of meaning. They are often repeated by the author throughout a chapter or book in order to reveal the point or purpose of the writing. Again, words that are repeated or are constant themes (such as love, covenant, sin or grace) are key clues to the authors intent in writing.

Pay attention to pronouns (he, she, we, they, I, you, it, our, etc.) as they often indicate a change of direction or emphasis. (e.g., when it changes from "He" says, to "you" say.) Note the synonyms which are different ways of referring to the same person, place, or thing. For instance, there are many names for God. These often hint at different character traits of the same entity, trying to teach us a little more about the subject. For instance, the name for God can be Elohim - meaning "the Powerful One," while the name Jehovah Jireh means "God is my Provider." Both are translated *God* in the English language.

LOOK FOR LISTS

Trivia Time: In movies, books and everyday speech, people often refer to "The Seven Deadly Sins" – where did that come from? Lists are often additional words used to describe a key word, but are also what is said about someone or something or related thoughts/instructions grouped together.

Lists are something you should develop as you study a particular topic throughout the Bible. For example, take a topic such as grace. Listing the characteristics of grace as provided by each use throughout Scripture will provide you with a much broader view of the whole meaning of grace. Such a list allows you to see the bigger picture and avoids incorrectly interpreting it on the basis of just one Scripture.

Watch For Contrasts And Comparisons

A contrast is a comparison of things that are different or opposite, such as light and darkness, proud and humble, and good and evil. The word often indicates a contrast to something just stated.

A comparison points out similarities and is most often indicated in the use of words such as like, and as. These small words are great eye-openers in the process of observation as they set the words on either side of them into their proper context.

Identify Terms Of Conclusion

Wherefore, therefore, for this reason, and finally, are terms of conclusion that usually follow an important thought in order to tell you how to personally apply the teaching. They're a bridge between the teaching and the application and often clearly spell out the proper meaning and context of the passage with no guesswork as to what it means.

Develop Your Own Chapter Themes

The printed chapter themes in most Bibles are more of an aid for finding a specific story or passage such as "Jesus Heals a Blind Man." They're not very descriptive of the spiritual topic or theme that reveals the lessons God is directing to your heart.

Nearly every Bible translation is available without such markings, usually in a wide margin edition conducive to making personal notes. *"The New Inductive Study Bible"* by Harvest House Publishers, for instance, builds this into several versions and even provides a place at the end of every book to record your personal chapter headings in order to see patterns and development of themes. But this can also easily be maintained on a separate sheet of paper.

NOTE EXPRESSIONS OF TIME

This is often the most overlooked part of observation. A crucial part of attaining the correct context is to understand when something has, is, or will happen.

Time is often directly indicated such as "during the reign of", "on the tenth day", "at the feast of", etc. Sometimes the context is as much about when, or its relationship to a past or present event, as it is the person, place, or thing mentioned.

Pay attention to words such as until, then, when, and after as they reveal the relationship of one event to another. This is of particular importance when studying the Gospels as you will begin to see that Jesus' acts and miracles are often an extension of the teaching He gave just before or after them. Throughout the Bible these words help connect actions with teaching, in the proper context.

These are the fundamentals and, to be sure, there are added guidelines for the proper observation applied to some of the different types of literature provided throughout the Bible such as psalms, songs, parables, allegories, etc.

But this will serve as the baseline throughout. Proper observation takes the guesswork out of interpretation and application. As stated previously, don't rush through observation because you want to get to interpretation or application more quickly. The latter are only properly achieved through patient and thorough observation.

Lesson 8

Step Two - Interpretation

ANYONE WHO ATTEMPTS to read the Bible will automatically be interpreting a text of Scripture. However, the Bible is not always easy to understand. Even when the text seems clear-cut, we may feel unsure that our interpretation is correct. I am sure that we all want to treat the Word of God with the respect it deserves, and we certainly don't want to read into it things that are not there. For these reasons, we need to apply the basic principles of hermeneutics— which is the science of interpretation.

For many believers, we already apply these principles just by using common sense. It is simply principles of good foundational reading. Though the Bible is a distinctive book in many ways, many of the rules for interpreting the Bible are rules for interpreting any book. The goal of our Bible reading and study is to find out what it means.

These seven rules can help us understand what God is saying to us through Scripture. These seven rules are not original and have been handed down through various professors and are taught today in various Bible colleges and seminaries. When I was at Philadelphia College of Bible, these rules were handed down to me and now I have the privilege of sharing these with you.

RULE 1 – LOOK FOR THE AUTHOR'S ENVISIONED MEANING

A mistake that is usually made in interpreting Scripture is to ask at the beginning of the process, "What does this passage mean to me?" Instead, during this second step, it is important to ask, "What was the author's intent when he wrote the passage?" This is the goal of interpretation.

Recognize that this principle admits that there is a meaning to a text! Today, there is a tendency to read relativity into the Scriptures and so, to admit "meaning" is very critical to interpretation. Many non-believing liberal interpreters of the Bible would suggest that the Bible has no set meaning, and is rather vague.

When we interpret the Bible we are looking for the author's original meaning, not imposing our own meaning on the text. As my professor in college would remind us as students, "when our interpretation disagrees with the authors' original interpretation, then our interpretation is wrong."

Each biblical passage has a set meaning intended by its author. Let me set an example from American History. If I would recite, " "Four score and seven years ago our fathers brought forth on this continent a new nation..." most of you would recognize that the author was our own President Abraham Lincoln, the 16th president of the United States and that it was an address given at Gettysburg on November 19, 1863 during the American Civil War. The purpose of this particular document was to unify the nation in the context of this war. So then, you can see, how important it is to **look for the author's envisioned meaning** and to understand the document.

It is the same way in the Scriptures. Paul, wrote 1 Corinthians in A.D. 55, from Ephesus during his third missionary journey. The recipients are this immature, struggling church at Corinth. Paul has just received a group of people from Corinth with questions from the church and reports of problems that are ongoing in the church. Paul's purpose, then, is to call the church to unity, and to call the church to maturity. He desires that once again they submit to the word of God's authority. Understanding those specific questions of historical context, such as, why the book was written, when the book was written, the purpose for which the book was written; these are critical questions for understanding the letter of 1 Corinthians.

Rule 2 – Read A Passage In Its Context

You've probably noticed that people can try to prove anything from the Bible that they desire. They can rip verses from the Bible or even major portions of the Bible and take them out at whim. That is fine if all you want to do is justify one's own predetermined ideas and lifestyles.

The key to understanding what the Bible says is to read it as it was first written, paragraph-by-paragraph. Each book of the Bible, written in its original Hebrew and Greek, was organized into paragraphs. Chapters and verses were added beginning in the 13th century, with a reference system added to help people find specific passages easier. The Geneva Bible (1599) was the first to begin each verse on a separate line, a practice that the King James Version (1611) eventually accepted. The bad side effect of this addition was that many readers began reading each verse separately, and ignored the context of the passages. Paragraphs provide context.

I want to encourage you to think in paragraphs. First, look for the single main idea in a paragraph. It is usually either in the first sentence or in the last sentence of the paragraph. Second, study how everything else in the paragraph supports the single main idea in that paragraph. Third, take time to observe how the paragraph fits into the entire book that you are studying. Refer to an online outline of the book, like those in many study Bibles, Bible dictionaries, Bible introductions, or Bible handbooks. Look at how your paragraph fits into the flow of the entire book.

Rule 3 – Identify The Literary Type Of The Passage

The Bible is filled with many literary types. It is a library of 66 books that were written over a period of 1500 years by many authors. As we've noted in prior chapters, these authors were inspired by the Holy Spirit in their thinking and writing. Therefore, the Bible is the inspired Word of God without error. It also has the human touch from its authors. Paul is different from Moses, who is different from Luke or Mark. So, their style and personalities are all different.

The Bible, then, is to be seen as literature, as is any book, filled with many kinds or types of language. It has Law, History, Wisdom, Poetry, Gospel, Epistles, Prophecy, and Apocalyptic Literature.

Let me give you just a few examples of the basic types:

- **<u>History</u>**: There are some great stories in the books of Genesis, Exodus, Numbers, Joshua, Judges, Nehemiah, Esther, Jonah, and Acts.
- **<u>Law</u>**: These are the commands of God given to us by way of Moses, in the books of Leviticus and Deuteronomy.
- **Wisdom:** Three books that are examples of books of wisdom are Job, Proverbs, and Ecclesiastes.
- **Poetry:** Three examples of prose and rhymes are Psalms, Song of Solomon, and Lamentations.
- **Prophecy:** There are a number of both major and minor prophets that are listed in the prophetic line. They are: Isaiah, Jeremiah, Ezekiel, Daniel, Hosea, Joel, Amos, Obadiah, Micah, Nahum, Habakkuk, Zephaniah, Haggai, Zechariah, and Malachi.
- **Apocalyptic:** The two most famous prophetic examples of Apocalyptic books in the Bible are Daniel and most of Revelation.
- **Parable:** These are the sayings of Jesus that are narrative and instructional, contained in the Gospels.

- **Epistle:** These are the letters written to a specific audience that are practical for us today such as Romans, Corinthians, Galatians, Ephesians, Philippians, Colossians, Thessalonians, Timothy, Titus, Philemon, Hebrews, James, Peter, John, and the first three chapters of Revelation.
- **Romance:** These are narrative, written also as love stories, such as Ruth and Song of Solomon.

Rule 4 – Consider The Historical And Cultural Background Of The Bible

The Bible was written in a time far distant from ours and in cultures quite strange to us. So as we try to discover the author's meaning, we must learn to read his writing as one of his contemporaries would. We must transport ourselves by means of our informed imagination back to the time of Moses, David, Solomon, or Paul.

But how do we do this? For most Bible readers, it means turning to commentaries and other helps. These books can give us insight into the cultural and historical backgrounds to the biblical books.

For instance, the Bible often depicts the Lord as riding a cloud (Psalm 18:7-15, 68:4, 104:3; Nahum 1:3). We might learn from a commentary that Israel's neighbors frequently pictured the god Baal riding a cloud of chariot into battle. As we place the biblical image in the light of the ancient Near East, we realize that God's cloud is a chariot that He rides into war. When we turn to the New Testament and see that Jesus also is a cloud-rider (Matthew 24:30, Revelation 1:7), we understand that this is not a white, fluffy cloud, but a storm cloud that He rides into judgment. Furthermore, we now sense that the use of the image was an appeal to those Israelites who worshipped the wrong god, Baal, to come back and worship the true cloud-rider, the Lord.

But what about a passage like Psalm 23? Can't we understand the imagery of a shepherd without recourse to the ancient world? We know what a shepherd does. He protects, guides, and takes care of his sheep. The answer is yes, and no. Shepherds in biblical times acted like shepherds in modern times in all these ways. However, unless we are aware of the use of the shepherd image in the ancient Near East, we will miss an important aspect of the psalm. The great kings of the Near East often referred to themselves as the "shepherds" of their people. Thus, as we read Psalm 23 in the light of its ancient background, we recover an important teaching of Psalm 23: the Lord is a royal shepherd.

Rule 5 – Consider The Grammar And Structure Of A Passage

The Bible was written in language form, and language has a certain structure and follows certain rules. Thereby, we must interpret the Bible in a manner consistent with the basic rules of language.

It is proper to start examining a passage by defining the words in it. Definitions are basic to understanding the passage as a whole, and it is important that the words be defined according to their original intent and not according to modern usage. To ensure accuracy, the exegete uses a precise English translation and Greek and Hebrew dictionaries.

Next, examine the grammatical relationships of the words in the passage. Try to find parallels to determine which ideas are primary and which are subordinate.

Third, what are the subjects, verbs, adjectives, prepositional phrases, etc. All these will help to determine the meaning of the author.

Rule 6 – Don't Interpret Scripture Through Your Own Lenses

All too often, we distort Scripture by allowing our experience to shape our understanding of Scripture rather than the other way around.

The point of Bible study is not to shape Scripture to agree with your subjective opinions or your experiences. Feelings can be very deceptive. Emotions can lie. Instead, discover God's timeless truth and let it shape your life. Study the Bible with an open heart and invite God to conform you to His will.

Rule 7 – Never Isolate One Passage From the Rest Of Scripture

When you are interpreting God's Word accurately, it is important that you do not accept a teaching simply because someone has used an isolated verse or two so support a theory. Those verses may have been taken out of context, or verses may have been overlooked that would have led to a different conclusion.

As you read the Word of God more extensively, one of the major rules of interpretation is that Scripture will never contradict Scripture. Remember, all Scripture is inspired by God. It is God-breathed. Therefore, Scripture will never contradict itself. Sometimes, though, it will be hard to reconcile questionable truth taught in Scripture.

A good example of this is the *Sovereignty of God* and the *responsibility of Man*. Don't take a teaching to an extreme that God doesn't. Simply take both truths by faith, as given in God's Word, even if it cannot be understood fully at the moment.

Another warning in the area of isolation is when certain para-theologians try to figure out when Christ will return through mathematics, even though the Scriptures tell us that "no one knows the time nor the hour when Christ will return" (Mark 13:32). Many times they manipulate and stretch passages in order to try to come up with some type of solution to their conclusion. They will bend and manipulate various passages in order to be the "first" to predict when Christ will return. Harold Camping back in 1988, sold 4 million copies of his book, *88 Reasons Why The Rapture Could Be In 1988*. When it didn't happen in 1988, he revised it 1989. When that didn't happen, there was yet another math revision to October 21, 2011. Finally for the first time, Harold Camping admitted that his prediction was faulty and until his death in 2013 refused to make any more predictions. However, his followers refused to put down their calculators and added October 7, 2015 to the list of the end of the world. And to the writing of this book, the latest date that I have been able to research, this group associated with Harold Camping has predicted that the end of the world will occur on May 20, 2018.

Oh, the danger of complicating the clear reading of Scripture. Mark says, "But about that day or hour no one knows, not even the angels in heaven, nor the Son, but only the Father" (Mark 13:32).

Conclusion

It is impossible to approach the Bible in a completely objective way. We all come to the Bible with questions, issues, troubles, and joys. Each of us also approaches the Bible from different cultural and social experiences. This truth contains great benefit and danger.

The benefit is that the Bible is relevant for every life. The danger, of course, is that we will warp God's Word in a way that it was never intended to be read.

There are three ways to avoid the danger while maximizing the benefits. The first is to follow the seven principles for understanding Scripture. These can keep you from reading your own thoughts into the Bible and help you discover the intention of the Author Himself.

The second is to read the Bible in community. That is, don't be a lone ranger in your Bible interpretation. Talk to others about what the Bible means to them and be open to their reading of the text. Read books by Christians from other walks of life and different cultural backgrounds. Finally, bathe your Scripture reading in prayer and ask the Holy Spirit to open your eyes to the truth found in the Word. Without the Spirit, we cannot understand God's Word (2 Corinthians 2:6-16).

Understanding Scripture does not have to be a daunting task. After all, the God who gave us His Word longs for us to understand it, even more than we do.

Lesson 9

Step Three – Application

You have now come to the third step of our learning in our Three Step process. And these three steps are really three questions that you can ask yourself every time you want to have a great Bible study. Before I get to this third step, I want to just do a quick review.

To set the stage, I want to emphasize that for you to be a growing Christian, it is vital for you to be in God's Word. It is God's Word that gives you revelation, truth and insight. It is His Word that speaks to us today. And we firmly believe today, as evangelical Christians that the Word of God is truth and it does not change. We can rest our weight and put our confidence in His Word. In fact, it becomes the measuring rod and the boundary for our lives. In other words, how do I know how I am supposed to live? By getting into God's Word. My interaction with God's Word is so critically important, because if I want to grow and mature in my faith, I need to be a man or a woman of the Word.

As I mentioned in the earlier chapters, there are three steps or three questions that you need to be asking. These are three steps that help you go deeper and gain a greater understanding of not only the passage, but a richer intimacy with God.

Step One - Observation - What Do I See In This Passage?

In this step we are asking the question, what does the text say. The purpose of this question is to get you to see what is in the passage itself. Sure, you've read it a couple times, but grab a piece of paper and pen and begin to list everything you see going on; it will be amazing how much you discover.

Step Two – Interpretation - What Does It Mean?

Once you've read the passage through several times and walked through the observation stage, you are ready to ask yourself: "What does it mean?" We are not asking, "what does it mean to ME?" Rather we are asking, "what did it mean to the original hearers/audience the author was writing to?" This is key! The author wasn't writing specifically to you, he was writing in a particular culture, with a particular thought process, with a particular reason in mind. So if you were in Corinth and received one of Paul's letters written to the Christians in that city, what did that passage mean to that group?

Now, once I have this concept, I can now move onto this third step which is application.

STEP THREE – APPLICATION - WHAT DOES IT CHANGE?

The object in this step is to ask, "how does it change my life?" The idea here, that for a good application, is not just to come up with a checklist of good ideas. But I am really laying myself before the Word of God saying, "Word of God examine my life!"

Does this concept or truth reflect in my life? For example, let's say the concept is "love your neighbor." I could quickly question myself and ask, "Do I really do that? I am just filled with an over-sensing love for them. I am consumed that they love Jesus. I am so delighted to get them into God's Word." And so, I'm taking this concept and I'm putting myself before God's Word and I'm allowing God's Word, like a two-edged sword to pierce my life, to bring revelation on how I'm supposed to live.

GOAL – LIFE TRANSFORMATION

The end result here is life transformation. We've all left Bible studies and left saying, "Great truth!" But if we never applied it to our lives, we always remain the same person. My desire is not to be the same person today that I was last week. I don't want to be the same man a year from now as I am today. I want a continual progression, transformation and movement into the realities into the fullness of all that Jesus wants to give me. I want Christ to take His Word and apply it into my life where the Word becomes the measuring rod for my life; where He is constantly bending me around God's Word.

God's Word does not bend. God takes my life, bends me and shapes me according to His unchanging Word.

Warnings To Beware

If you do Bible study and you decide not to apply God's Word, you will be left with stagnation. James told his readers, *"Do not merely listen to the word, and so deceive yourselves. Do what it says"* (James 1:22). James compared the Bible to a mirror, for as we look into the Word of God, we see ourselves reflected in it.

We see our blemishes.

We see how we need to touch up our lives in God's sight.

Some people walk away from God's mirror without making the needed changes. Recently, in my own life, I experienced this very area. I had to take a really strong look into the mirror and see the blemishes in my own life and not like what I saw and repent. I am so happy for the next part of the verse which says, *"But,"* said James, *"...whoever looks intently into the perfect law that gives freedom, and continues in it—not forgetting what they have heard, but doing it—they will be blessed in what they do"* (verse 25).

This was also the theme of the Sermon on the Mount. Disappointed at the hypocrisy in His day, Jesus condemned the religionists who studied the Old Testament, but never got around to applying its message. In His sermon in Matthew 5–7, Christ urged life-changing obedience to His words and concluded with the story of the two builders. One built a house on a rock, the other on sand.

The first man's house withstood the storm, but the house on the sand collapsed. What was the difference?

> *"Therefore everyone who hears these words of mine and puts them into practice is like a wise man who built his house on the rock"*
>
> (MATTHEW 7:24)

> *But everyone who hears these words of mine and does not put them into practice is like a foolish man who built his house on sand"*
>
> (MATTHEW 7:26)

Both men heard the words of Jesus. Both were in His audience that day, listening with great admiration. Both were Bible students of His Words. But one put the truth into practice, while the other nodded politely and continued through his life as usual.

QUESTIONS TO ASK

When we study the Bible, then, whether in a group or on our own, we should always consider what it says, what it means, and what it means for us.

Don't stop at satisfying your mental curiosity. Lots of people, for example, are fascinated by the study of the end times, the Rapture of the Church, the Great Tribulation, and the Second Coming of

Christ. I always stress that God hasn't given prophecy just to satisfy our curiosity, but to encourage us to holy living and evangelism. Our beliefs should regulate our behavior. Knowing Christ is coming tomorrow should affect the urgency of obedience today.

Howard Hendricks has put together in his book, *Living by the Book* a variety of questions that are excellent questions to ask when trying to apply a passage of Scripture.

- *Is there an example for me to follow?*
- *Is there a promise for me to claim?*
- *Is there a prayer for me to repeat?*
- *Is there a command for me to obey?*
- *Is there a doctrinal error for me to correct?*
- *Is there a challenge for me to face?*

When you ask yourself those questions while studying the Bible, the Lord will show you the answers. When you ask those questions while teaching the Bible, your listeners will come to realize the Bible wasn't merely given to *inform* us but to *transform* us.

Lessons To Learn

The Bible is full of stories. As we read our way through God's Word, there are stories about understanding God's will, as in the life of Abraham and Sarah. Or we comprehend the dangers of lust, such as in the lives of David and Bathsheba. We read about Paul's conversion and salvation.

The lives of Bible characters are living example in which the truths of the Bible are applied, as are our own lives.

Finally, it is important that we realize that we are not alone in applying God's Word to our lives. God has filled us with His Spirit (John 14:16-17) who speaks to us, leading and guiding us into all truth (John 16:13). Because of this, the Apostle Paul tells believers to "walk by the Spirit" (Galatians 5:16), for He is a our Help in times when we need help (Psalm 46:1).

The Spirit will always guide us into following the will of God, instructing us to do what is right (Ezekiel 36:26-28; Philippians 2:13).

So then, our part is to hide the Word of God in our hearts and obey (submit) to the Holy Spirit as He draws that Word out of us.

Lesson 10

Applying God's Word – Staying Away From Extremism

As I stated in Lesson Eight, the goal of interpretation is to discover the original intent of the author, that is, what he had in mind when he wrote the Words of God. Yet, when the time comes to apply God's Word, the Bible student will have to bridge the gap of the ancient world to the present world. So, how do you and I stay away from extremism? What can we do to guard ourselves from erroneous applications? What's to ensure us to staying practical, yet true to God's Word?

There are no set guarantees, yet there are three guidelines that I would like to share with the reader.

1. Your Conclusions And Applications Should Correlate With The General Teaching Of Scripture.

This principle brings us back to comparing Scripture with Scripture. As you state a principle from a particular passage, think about passages that reinforce that truth. For instance, Proverbs 20:2 says, "A king's wrath strikes terror like the roar of a lion; those who anger him forfeit their lives." Some believers have interpreted that this means that we should have unbridled allegiance to the government. I would be comfortable in saying that we should have "respect" for authority because it is backed up in other passages such as Romans 13:1-7; and 1 Peter 2:13-17, but not an "unbridled" allegiance. There are instances where we must obey God rather than man (Acts 5:29). Yet, I can feel confident in applying Proverbs 20:2 in this manner.

I remember a young man and young lady coming into my office telling me that it was fine for them to live together, even though they weren't married. The young man was a believer and the young lady was not. Various passages came to mind about abstinence until marriage (2 Timothy 2:22), as well as marrying a person who is an unbeliever (2 Corinthians 6:14-18). Our conclusions and applications of Scripture should always correlate with the general teaching of Scripture.

2. Culture Should Always Bow To Scripture.

While cultural change might tempt us to jettison those interpretive principles, we must always go back to our need to faithfully and responsibly interpret Scripture, with Scripture as our starting point for all matters of faith and practice.

While it's becoming more and more commonplace for Christians to view and interpret Scripture through the eyes of our culture, we need to be doing the opposite as we view, interpret, and respond to culture through the eyes of Scripture.

John Stott, once said, *"It's not difficult to be contemporary if you don't care to be Biblical, and it's not difficult to be Biblical if you don't care to be contemporary. But to be Biblical and contemporary – that's an art."*

There are several "rules of thumbs" that can help in maneuvering through the landmines of culture change.

First, if there are direct commands from Scripture, then the issue is resolved. If the word of God gives a command, then that should settle it in the mind of the believer. For instance, the Ten Commandments are not Ten Suggestions. Just in case you may not remember them, here they are:

- Do not have any other god before God.
- Do not make yourself an idol.
- Do not take the Lord's name in vain.
- Remember the Sabbath Day and keep it holy.
- Honor thy mother and father.
- Do not murder.

- Do not commit adultery.
- Do not steal.

We do not have the option to "cut out" or "tear out" major portions of the Bible because they may not correlate with our cultural view. Remember that the Bible was written over 2000 years of history, and a lot of cultural change occurred during those years, yet the Word of God stood time.

Second, we must never change the truth to fit the cultural agenda. Rather, we must change our application of the truth in light of our needs. Let me explain. In Genesis 2:24, God set up the marriage institution. He said, *"That is why a man leaves his father and mother and is united to his wife, and they become one flesh."*

What must Adam and Eve's marriage have looked like before the Fall? Imagine the level of communication, trust, partnership and intimacy they must have experienced. But then they sinned. But now, they have a new set of dynamics to contend with – mistrust, selfishness, pride and lust. Yet, God leaves intact the expectation to live as one flesh. That's a whole new context.

Jump ahead to Moses as he relates the Genesis account to the people of Israel. They are coming out of Egypt where polygamy is common. For that matter, even Israel's own patriarchs had concubines. What does a one-flesh relationship look like, given that legacy? Again, a change in context.

Later, Paul writes to the Ephesians. Ephesus was the tourist capital of the world and perhaps the wealthiest of all the Roman cities. But the time that Paul came on the scene in Acts 19, marriage had fallen into a sorry state, particularly among the wealthy. Remarking on the women of his day, the Roman philosopher Seneca said, "*They divorce in order to re-marry. They marry in order to divorce.*" His equally cynical son defined a faithful married woman as one who only had two lovers.

Paul had already caused one full scale riot in Ephesus with this new and strange teaching (Acts 19:23-41). Now, he astounds the young Ephesian believers with his letter. Like Jesus, he quotes Genesis 2:24 and then says, "*Husbands, each of you also must love his wife as he loves himself, and the wife must respect her husband*" (Ephesians 5:33). How does a couple pursue a one-flesh relationship in the context of first-century Ephesus?

This is the same question that we must face today. Whether it is adultery, homosexuality, or pre-marital sex, this same question must be confronted with having the Bible as the authority above culture.

The point is that the Word of God is eternal and unchanging, but our world is not. Therefore, living out God's truth demands that we plug into our particular set of circumstances. Again, we do not change the truth to fit our cultural agenda. Rather, we can change our application of the truth in light of our needs.

3. THE END OF BIBLE STUDY SHOULD LEAD YOU TO A COURSE OF ACTION

I think that we've all been in Bible Studies or Small Group meetings where we have studied God's Word, and at the end there was a closing prayer, and you walked away thinking, what was the purpose? What was the "take away" from the passage?

HOW TO STUDY YOUR BIBLE

It is very easy to be hypothetical and to be theologically speculative. That was the problem that Paul ran into in Athens (Acts 17:21). The people there loved to sit around and shoot the breeze. But God's Word was not given to tease our curiosity, but to transform our lives. That's why the application step is so important to Bible study.

I remember one time, during one of the counseling sessions at church, I shared with a man the concept in the Word of God to serve one another, and that included serving his wife. He was from a different generation where it didn't come easy for him to think in those terms.

>He was the man of the house.
>>He was the provider.
>>>His job was to go out and make a living.
>>>>His wife was to stay at home and take care of him.

When he got the concept, it revolutionized his marriage.

This may not sound like much for you, but for this man, it was a completely new way of thinking. It represented a life-change. He took a major step in his marriage in response to a Biblical principle.

Final Thoughts

A Call For A New Reformation

Take a look around our world. There may be a need for a new call for a reformation, both for our culture and for the Church. We must return to the Bible as our absolute authority.

The church is being bombarded by liberalism, evolutionism, Gnosticism, Mormonism, Islam, New Age, Moral Relativism, abortion, and the list goes on.

In 2 Corinthians 11:3, the Apostle Paul, under the inspiration of the Holy Spirit, warns us about this ever-present danger: *"But I am afraid that just as Eve was deceived by the serpent's cunning, your minds may somehow be led astray from your sincere and pure devotion to Christ."* Paul, in essence is warning Christians that Satan will continue to sway people using the same methods as he did with Eve. Satan will try to seduce people away from a simple devotion to Christ and His Word.

Historical Challenges

This battle against God's Word has manifested itself in every era of history.

Paul faced skeptics on every side, who questioned the clear proclamation of God's Word. In its early centuries, Christianity fought several challenges to the authority of the Scriptures, including Gnosticism, which taught that man was his own god. Modern issues like the age of dinosaurs or carbon dating are merely new manifestations of age-old attacks on God's Word.

In the sixteenth century, the sale of indulgences by the church for forgiveness of sin and release from the pains of Purgatory, marked a climax in the elevation of human thinking above God's Word. Martin Luther nailed his 95 theses to the door of the Wittenberg Church, challenging indulgences. This act sparked a debate about the ultimate authority of the Bible above the Church and it essentially began the Reformation.

Others joined this reform movement. The Western world was dramatically changed, as Bibles and tracts were printed on the presses and distributed widely.

In the eighteenth and nineteenth centuries, the attack against the Bible intensified. New speculation about the age of the earth and evolution raised questions about the accuracy of the Bible. These core issues can be seen in the Scopes trial (1925) which opened the door for teaching the theory of evolution in the public schools.

Is A New Reformation Needed Today?

Today, a new reformation may be needed. I know that there are some that are using this "cry" for a reformation back to the Roman Catholic church. But that is not my call.

It's time for a new generation of reformers to stand up and call the church back to trust in God's Word where it is most under attack. It is time for believers to once again open up and begin to read and study the Scriptures they claim to believe in. The entire Word of God.

My desire is that you would long for a greater, deeper understanding of Christ and His Word as you have read this book. By studying the Bible it will transform the way you think and live. By studying the Bible, God Himself will become your Teacher as you learn how to hang on His Words and discover the truth for yourself. His Words will be life changing!

So, charge ahead, reformers!
>Dig into God's Word!
>>Learn the tools needed and grow! May God richly bless you as you discover through His Holy Spirit the full knowledge of His Words.

Made in the USA
Middletown, DE
22 August 2017